Keep It Moving

Journal

Keep It Moving Journal
Copyright © 2023 Kathy L. Cunningham

Scripture quotations in this book are taken from the Holy Bible, New King James Version® unless otherwise noted in the text. Copyright ©1982 by Thomas Nelson. Used by permission. All rights reserved. Scripture quotations marked AMP are taken from the Amplified Bible. Copyright ©2015 by The Lockman Foundation. Used by permission. Scripture quotations marked KJV are taken from the King James Version of the Bible, Public Domain. Scripture quotations marked MSG are taken from the Message Bible. Copyright ©2002. Used by permission of NavPress Publishing Group. Scripture quotations marked NASB are taken from the New American Standard Bible. Copyright ©1995 by The Lockman Foundation. Used by permission. Scripture quotations marked NIV are taken from the Holy Bible, New International Version®, NIV® Copyright ©2011 by Biblica, Inc.® Used by permission. All rights reserved worldwide.

All rights reserved under International Copyright Law. No part of this journal may be reproduced or transmitted in any form or by any means without written permission of the Publisher, except for the inclusion of brief quotations in a review.

Cover design by TLH Designs, Chicago, IL
www.lovetlhayden.com

Published by:
Keep It Moving…You Have a Destiny
Fredericksburg, VA 22404

Published in the United States of America.

ISBN 978-0-578-62082-4

THIS JOURNAL BELONGS TO:

_____
_____
_____

DATE:

_____

Keep It Moving...You Have a Destiny

I will give thanks to You, for I am fearfully and wonderfully made;
Wonderful are Your works, And my soul knows it very well.
Psalm 139:14 (NASB)

_____
_____
_____
_____
_____
_____
_____
_____
_____
_____
_____
_____
_____
_____
_____
_____
_____
_____
_____
_____

I can do all things through Christ which strengthens me.
Philippians 4:13

_____
_____
_____
_____
_____
_____
_____
_____
_____
_____
_____
_____
_____
_____
_____
_____
_____
_____
_____
_____
_____
_____

In all your ways acknowledge Him, and He shall direct your paths.
Proverbs 3:6

"For I know the plans I have for you," declares the L*ORD*, *"plans to prosper you and not to harm you, plans to give you hope and a future."*
Jeremiah 29:11 (NIV)

Then the Lord answered me and said, "Write the vision nd make it plain on tablets, that he may run who reads it. Habakkuk 2:2

_____
_____
_____
_____
_____
_____
_____
_____
_____
_____
_____
_____
_____
_____
_____
_____
_____
_____
_____
_____
_____
_____

Commit to the LORD whatever you do, and He will establish your plans.
Proverbs 16:3 (NIV)

For the vision is yet for the appointed time; It hastens toward the goal and it will not fail. Though it tarries, wait for it; For it will certainly come, it will not delay. Habakkuk 2:3 (NASB)

_____
_____
_____
_____
_____
_____
_____
_____
_____
_____
_____
_____
_____
_____
_____
_____
_____
_____
_____
_____
_____

And I will restore to you the years that the locust hath eaten, the canker-worm, and the caterpillar, and the palmer-worm, my great army which I sent among you. Joel 2:25 (KJV)

And ye shall eat in plenty and be satisfied, and shall praise the name of Jehovah your God, that hath dealt wondrously with you; and my people shall never be put to shame. Joel 2:26

*But we have this precious treasure [the good news about salvation]
in [unworthy] earthen vessels [of human frailty], so that the
grandeur and surpassing greatness of the power will be [shown to be] from
God [His sufficiency] and not from ourselves.*
2 Corinthians 4:7 (AMP)

_____
_____
_____
_____
_____
_____
_____
_____
_____
_____
_____
_____
_____
_____
_____
_____
_____

The earth is the Lord's, and the fulness thereof; the world, and they that dwell therein. Psalm 24:1 (KJV)

*"...In the same way, I will not cause pain without allowing something new to be born." The L*ORD *says this: "I promise that if I cause you the pain of birth, I will not stop you from having your new nation." Your God said this. Isaiah 66:9 (ERV)*

_____

_____
_____
_____
_____
_____
_____
_____
_____
_____
_____
_____
_____
_____
_____
_____
_____
_____
_____
_____
_____

Every good gift and every perfect gift is from above, and cometh down from the Father of lights, with whom is no variableness, neither shadow of turning. James 1:17 (KJV)

Because it is written, "Be holy, for I am holy." 1 Peter 1:16

_____
_____
_____
_____
_____
_____
_____
_____
_____
_____
_____
_____
_____
_____
_____
_____
_____
_____
_____
_____
_____
_____
_____

*For I am the L*ORD *who brings you up out of the land of Egypt, to be your God: ye shall therefore be holy, for I am holy. Leviticus 11:45*

For the wages of sin is death; but the gift of God is eternal life through Jesus Christ our Lord. Romans 6:23

_____
_____
_____
_____
_____
_____
_____
_____
_____
_____
_____
_____
_____
_____
_____
_____
_____
_____
_____
_____
_____
_____
_____
_____

And you know that He was manifested to take away our sins, and in Him there is no sin. 1 John 3:5

He delivered me from my strong enemy, From those who hated me, For they were too strong for me. They confronted me in the day of my calamity, But the L<small>ORD</small> was my support. Psalm 18:17-18

___

___

___

___

___

___

___

___

___

___

___

___

___

___

___

___

___

___

___

___

___

You are my hiding place; You shall preserve me from trouble;
You shall surround me with songs of deliverance. Selah. Psalm 32:7

_____
_____
_____
_____
_____
_____
_____
_____
_____
_____
_____
_____
_____
_____
_____
_____
_____
_____
_____
_____
_____
_____

I will instruct you and teach you in the way you should go; I will guide you with my eye. Psalm 32:8

*The L*ORD *is my rock, and my fortress, and my deliverer; my God, my strength, in whom I will trust; my buckler, and the horn of my salvation, and my high tower. Psalm 18:2 (KJV)*

*I will call upon the L*ORD*, who is worthy to be praised: so shall I be saved from mine enemies. Psalm 18:3 (KJV)*

The LORD is my shepherd; I shall not want. He makes me to lie down in green pastures: He leads me beside the still waters. He restores my soul: He leads me in the paths of righteousness for His name's sake. Yea, though I walk through the valley of the shadow of death, I will fear no evil: for You are with me; Your rod and Your staff, they comfort me. You prepare a table before me in the presence of my enemies: You anoint my head with oil; my cup runs over. Surely goodness and mercy shall follow me all the days of my life: and I will dwell in the house of the LORD forever. Psalm 23

_____
_____
_____
_____
_____
_____
_____
_____
_____
_____
_____
_____
_____

Thus says the LORD: Let not the wise man glory in his wisdom, let not the mighty man glory in his might, nor let the rich man glory in his riches: But let him who glories glory in this, that he understands and knows Me, that I am the LORD, exercising lovingkindness, judgment, and righteousness, in the earth. For in these I delight, says the LORD. Jeremiah 9:23-24

_____
_____
_____
_____
_____
_____
_____
_____
_____
_____
_____
_____
_____
_____
_____
_____
_____

Oh, taste and see that the LORD is good; blessed is the man who trusts in Him! Psalm 34:8

I cried unto the L<small>ORD</small> with my voice; with my voice unto the L<small>ORD</small> did I make my supplication. Psalm 142:1 (KJV)

_____
_____
_____
_____
_____
_____
_____
_____
_____
_____
_____
_____
_____
_____
_____
_____
_____
_____
_____
_____
_____
_____
_____
_____

O God, You are my God; early will I seek You; my soul thirsts for You; my flesh longs for You in a dry and thirsty land where there is no water.
Psalm 63:1

_____
_____
_____
_____
_____
_____
_____
_____
_____
_____
_____
_____
_____
_____
_____
_____
_____
_____
_____
_____

The thief cometh not, but for to steal, and to kill, and to destroy: I am come that they might have life, and that they might have it more abundantly. John 10:10 (KJV)

_____
_____
_____
_____
_____
_____
_____
_____
_____
_____
_____
_____
_____
_____
_____
_____
_____
_____
_____

*I will bless the L*ORD *at all times; His praise shall continually be in my mouth. Psalm 34:1*

_____
_____
_____
_____
_____
_____
_____
_____
_____
_____
_____
_____
_____
_____
_____
_____
_____
_____
_____
_____
_____
_____
_____
_____
_____

For whatsoever things were written aforetime were written for our learning, that we through patience and comfort of the scriptures might have hope. Romans 15:4

_____
_____
_____
_____
_____
_____
_____
_____
_____
_____
_____
_____
_____
_____
_____
_____
_____
_____
_____

You shall be My people, and I will be your God. Jeremiah 30:22

And my God shall supply all your need according to His riches in glory by Christ Jesus. Philippians 4:19

Therefore I say unto you, Take no thought for your life, what ye shall eat, or what ye shall drink; nor yet for your body, what ye shall put on. Is not the life more than meat, and the body than raiment?
Matthew 6:25 (KJV)

_____
_____
_____
_____
_____
_____
_____
_____
_____
_____
_____
_____
_____
_____
_____
_____
_____
_____
_____
_____
_____

But ye are a chosen generation, a royal priesthood, an holy nation, a peculiar people; that ye should shew forth the praises of Him who hath called you out of darkness into his marvellous light. 1 Peter 2:9 (KJV)

But they that wait upon the L<small>ORD</small> shall renew their strength; they shall mount up with wings as eagles; they shall run, and not be weary; and they shall walk, and not faint. Isaiah 40:31

_____
_____
_____
_____
_____
_____
_____
_____
_____
_____
_____
_____
_____
_____
_____
_____
_____
_____
_____
_____
_____

No weapon formed against you shall prosper, and every tongue which rises against you in judgment You shall condemn. This is the heritage of the servants of the LORD, and their righteousness is from Me, says the LORD. Isaiah 54:17

For God so loved the world, that He gave His only begotten Son, that whosoever believeth in Him should not perish, but have everlasting life.
John 3:16 (KJV)

For He shall give His angels charge over you, to keep you in all your ways.
Psalm 91:11

*There is therefore now no condemnation to those who are in Christ Jesus,
who do not walk according to the flesh, but according to the Spirit.
Romans 8:1*

_____
_____
_____
_____
_____
_____
_____
_____
_____
_____
_____
_____
_____
_____
_____
_____
_____
_____
_____
_____
_____
_____

By Him therefore let us offer the sacrifice of praise to God continually, that is, the fruit of our lips giving thanks to His name.
Hebrews 13:15 (KJV)

But seek first the Kingdom of God and His righteousness, and all these things shall be added to you. Matthew 6:33

_____
_____
_____
_____
_____
_____
_____
_____
_____
_____
_____
_____
_____
_____
_____
_____
_____
_____
_____
_____
_____

Therefore, if anyone is in Christ, he is a new creation; old things have passed away; behold, all things have become new. 2 Corinthians 5:17

_____
_____
_____
_____
_____
_____
_____
_____
_____
_____
_____
_____
_____
_____
_____
_____
_____
_____
_____
_____
_____

Not that I speak in respect of want: for I have learned, in whatsoever state I am, therewith to be content. I know both how to be abased, and I know how to abound: every where and in all things I am instructed both to be full and to be hungry, both to abound and to suffer need.
Philippians 4:11-12 (KJV)

It is God who arms me with strength and makes my way perfect. He makes my feet like the feet of deer and sets me on my high places. He teaches my hands to make war, so that my arms can bend a bow of bronze. You have also given me the shield of Your salvation; Your right hand has held me up, Your gentleness has made me great. You enlarged my path under me, so my feet did not slip. Psalm 18:32-36

_____
_____
_____
_____
_____
_____
_____
_____
_____
_____
_____
_____
_____
_____
_____
_____
_____

But let patience have her perfect work, that you may be perfect and entire, wanting nothing. James 1:4 (KJV)

*These things I have spoken to you, that in Me you may have peace.
In the world you will have tribulation; but be of good cheer, I have
overcome the world. John 16:33*

Do you not know that those who run in a race all run, but one receives the prize? Run in such a way that you may obtain it.
1 Corinthians 9:24

_____
_____
_____
_____
_____
_____
_____
_____
_____
_____
_____
_____
_____
_____
_____
_____
_____
_____

For it is God which worketh in you both to will and to do of His good pleasure. Philippians 2:13

Death and life are in the power of the tongue: and they that love it shall eat the fruit thereof. Proverbs 18:21

Now faith is the substance of things hoped for, the evidence of things not seen. Hebrews 11:1

But without faith it is impossible to please Him, for he who comes to God must believe that He is, and that He is a rewarder of those who diligently seek Him. Hebrews 11:6

_____
_____
_____
_____
_____
_____
_____
_____
_____
_____
_____
_____
_____
_____
_____
_____
_____
_____
_____
_____
_____

He said to them, "But who do you say that I am?" Matthew 16:15

Verily, verily, I say unto you, He that believeth on me, the works that I do shall he do also; and greater works than these shall he do; because I go unto My Father. John 14:12 (KJV)

_____
_____
_____
_____
_____
_____
_____
_____
_____
_____
_____
_____
_____
_____
_____
_____
_____
_____
_____
_____

Stand fast therefore in the liberty by which Christ has made us free, and do not be entangled again with a yoke of bondage. Galatians 5:1

_____
_____
_____
_____
_____
_____
_____
_____
_____
_____
_____
_____
_____
_____
_____
_____
_____
_____
_____
_____

Humble yourselves therefore under the mighty hand of God, that He may exalt you in due time: Casting all your care upon Him; for He cares for you. 1 Peter 5:6-7

_____
_____
_____
_____
_____
_____
_____
_____
_____
_____
_____
_____
_____
_____
_____
_____
_____
_____
_____
_____
_____

But the very hairs of your head are all numbered. Do not fear therefore; you are of more value than many sparrows. Luke 12:7

There remains therefore a rest for the people of God. Hebrews 4:9

_____
_____
_____
_____
_____
_____
_____
_____
_____
_____
_____
_____
_____
_____
_____
_____
_____
_____
_____
_____
_____
_____

For he who has entered His rest has himself also ceased from his works as God did from His. Hebrews 4:10

Lead me in Your truth and teach me, for You are the God of my salvation; on You I wait all the day. Psalm 25:5

_____
_____
_____
_____
_____
_____
_____
_____
_____
_____
_____
_____
_____
_____
_____
_____
_____
_____
_____
_____
_____
_____

For we wrestle not against flesh and blood, but against principalities, against powers, against the rulers of the darkness of this world, against spiritual wickedness in high places. Ephesians 6:12

_____
_____
_____
_____
_____
_____
_____
_____
_____
_____
_____
_____
_____
_____
_____
_____
_____
_____
_____
_____
_____

Let us labour therefore to enter into that rest, lest any man fall after the same example of unbelief. Hebrews 4:11 (KJV)

And thou shalt love the Lord thy God with all thy heart, and with all thy soul, and with all thy mind, and with all thy strength: this is the first commandment. Mark 12:30 (KJV)

_____
_____
_____
_____
_____
_____
_____
_____
_____
_____
_____
_____
_____
_____
_____
_____
_____
_____
_____
_____
_____

Casting down imaginations, and every high thing that exalts itself against the knowledge of God, and bringing into captivity every thought to the obedience of Christ. 2 Corinthians 10:5

_____
_____
_____
_____
_____
_____
_____
_____
_____
_____
_____
_____
_____
_____
_____
_____
_____
_____
_____
_____
_____
_____
_____

Wherefore He is able also to save them to the uttermost that come unto God by Him, seeing He ever lives to make intercession for them.
Hebrews 7:25

_____
_____
_____
_____
_____
_____
_____
_____
_____
_____
_____
_____
_____
_____
_____
_____
_____
_____
_____
_____

*For who has known the mind of the Lord, that he may instruct Him?
But we have the mind of Christ. 1 Corinthians 2:16*

_____
_____
_____
_____
_____
_____
_____
_____
_____
_____
_____
_____
_____
_____
_____
_____
_____
_____
_____
_____
_____
_____
_____

"These things I have spoken to you, that in Me you may have peace. In the world you will have tribulation; but be of good cheer, I have overcome the world." John 16:33

_____
_____
_____
_____
_____
_____
_____
_____
_____
_____
_____
_____
_____
_____
_____
_____
_____
_____
_____
_____

So Jesus answered and said to them, "Have faith in God. Mark 11:22

But the hour is coming, and now is, when the true worshippers will worship the Father in spirit and truth; for the Father is seeking such to worship Him. John 4:23

God is a Spirit: and they that worship Him must worship Him in spirit and in truth. John 4:24

For I know that my Redeemer lives, and that He shall stand at last on the earth. Job 19:25

Why art thou cast down, O my soul? and why art thou disquieted within me? hope thou in God: for I shall yet praise Him, who is the health of my countenance, and my God. Psalm 42:11 (KJV)

_____
_____
_____
_____
_____
_____
_____
_____
_____
_____
_____
_____
_____
_____
_____
_____
_____

Be still and know that I am God: I will be exalted among the heathen, I will be exalted in the earth. Psalm 46:10

And we know that all things work together for good to those who love God, to those who are the called according to His purpose. Romans 8:28

But as it is written: Eye has not seen, nor ear heard, nor have entered into the heart of man the things which God has prepared for those who love Him. 1 Corinthians 2:9

Behold, the former things are come to pass, and new things do I declare: before they spring forth I tell you of them. Isaiah 42:9

Oh, fear the L<small>ORD</small>, you His saints! There is no want to those who fear Him. Psalm 34:9

I can do all things through Christ who strengthens me. Philippians 4:13

Thine, O L̲o̲r̲d̲ is the greatness, and the power, and the glory, and the victory, and the majesty: for all that is in the heaven and in the earth is thine; thine is the kingdom, O L̲o̲r̲d̲, and thou art exalted as head above all. 1 Chronicles 29:11 (KJV)

_____
_____
_____
_____
_____
_____
_____
_____
_____
_____
_____
_____
_____
_____
_____
_____
_____

Both riches and honour come of thee, and thou reignest over all; and in thine hand is power and might; and in thine hand it is to make great, and to give strength unto all. 1 Chronicles 29:12 (KJV)

_____
_____
_____
_____
_____
_____
_____
_____
_____
_____
_____
_____
_____
_____
_____
_____
_____
_____
_____
_____
_____

For with God nothing shall be impossible. Luke 1:37

Now thanks be unto God, which always causes us to triumph in Christ, and makes manifest the savour of His knowledge by us in every place.
2 Corinthians 2:14 (KJV)

But the fruit of the Spirit is love, joy, peace, longsuffering, gentleness, goodness, faith, Meekness, temperance: against such there is no law. Galatians 5:22-23 (KJV)

_____
_____
_____
_____
_____
_____
_____
_____
_____
_____
_____
_____
_____
_____
_____
_____
_____
_____
_____
_____

O death, where is thy sting? O grave, where is thy victory? The sting of death is sin; and the strength of sin is the law. But thanks be to God, which giveth us the victory through our Lord Jesus Christ.
1 Corinthians 15:55-57 (KJV)

_____
_____
_____
_____
_____
_____
_____
_____
_____
_____
_____
_____
_____
_____
_____
_____
_____
_____
_____

Search me, O God, and know my heart: try me, and know my thoughts: And see if there be any wicked way in me and lead me in the way everlasting. Psalm 139:23-24 (KJV)

But He was wounded for our transgressions, He was bruised for our iniquities: the chastisement of our peace was upon Him; and with His stripes we are healed. Isaiah 53:5

_____
_____
_____
_____
_____
_____
_____
_____
_____
_____
_____
_____
_____
_____
_____
_____
_____
_____
_____
_____

Peace I leave with you, My peace I give to you; not as the world gives do I give to you. Let not your heart be troubled, neither let it be afraid. John 14:27

_____
_____
_____
_____
_____
_____
_____
_____
_____
_____
_____
_____
_____
_____
_____
_____
_____
_____
_____
_____

I am the door. If anyone enters by Me, he will be saved, and will go in and out, and find pasture. John 10:9

_____
_____
_____
_____
_____
_____
_____
_____
_____
_____
_____
_____
_____
_____
_____
_____
_____
_____
_____
_____
_____
_____
_____
_____

A double minded man is unstable in all his ways. James 1:8 (KJV)

_____
_____
_____
_____
_____
_____
_____
_____
_____
_____
_____
_____
_____
_____
_____
_____
_____
_____
_____
_____

Keep back thy servant also from presumptuous sins; let them not have dominion over me: then shall I be upright, and I shall be innocent from the great transgression. Psalm 19:13 (KJV)

Let the words of my mouth, and the meditation of my heart be acceptable in Your sight, O L̃o̴ʀ̃ᴅ, my strength, and my Redeemer. Psalm 19:14

_____
_____
_____
_____
_____
_____
_____
_____
_____
_____
_____
_____
_____
_____
_____
_____
_____
_____
_____
_____
_____
_____

But Jesus turned him about, and when He saw her, He said, Daughter, be of good comfort; thy faith hath made thee whole. And the woman was made whole from that hour. Matthew 9:22 (KJV)

*"For My thoughts are not your thoughts, nor are your ways My ways,"
says the L*ORD*. "For as the heavens are higher than the earth, so are My
ways higher than your ways, and My thoughts than your thoughts."
Isaiah 55:8-9*

_____
_____
_____
_____
_____
_____
_____
_____
_____
_____
_____
_____
_____
_____
_____
_____
_____

Trust in the Lord with all your heart and lean not on your own understanding; in all your ways acknowledge Him, and He shall direct thy paths. Proverbs 3:5-6

_____
_____
_____
_____
_____
_____
_____
_____
_____
_____
_____
_____
_____
_____
_____
_____
_____
_____
_____
_____
_____
_____

Do not be deceived, God is not mocked; for whatever a man sows, that he will also reap. Galatians 6:7

_____
_____
_____
_____
_____
_____
_____
_____
_____
_____
_____
_____
_____
_____
_____
_____
_____
_____
_____
_____

I the L<small>ORD</small> search the heart, I try the reins, even to give every man according to his ways, and according to the fruit of his doings.
Jeremiah 17:10

_____
_____
_____
_____
_____
_____
_____
_____
_____
_____
_____
_____
_____
_____
_____
_____
_____
_____

*Be still, and know that I am God: I will be exalted among the nations,
I will be exalted in the earth! Psalm 46:10*

The Virtuous Woman

A good woman is hard to find, and worth far more than diamonds. Her husband trusts her without reserve, and never has reason to regret it. Never spiteful, she treats him generously all her life long. She shops around for the best yarns and cottons and enjoys knitting and sewing. She's like a trading ship that sails to faraway places and brings back exotic surprises. She's up before dawn, preparing breakfast for her family and organizing her day.... Her clothes are well-made and elegant, and she always faces tomorrow with a smile. When she speaks she has something worthwhile to say, and she always says it kindly. She keeps an eye on everyone in her household and keeps them all busy and productive. Her children respect and bless her; her husband joins in with words of praise: "Many women have done wonderful things, but you've outclassed them all!" Charm can mislead and beauty soon fades. The woman to be admired and praised is the woman who lives in the Fear-of-God. Give her everything she deserves! Festoon her life with praises!

Proverbs 31:10-31 (MSG)

About

"Keep it Moving…
You Have a Destiny"

"Keep It Moving… You Have a Destiny" (KIM) empowers and encourages women to be all that God has called them to be, realizing that they have purpose and destiny. Sometimes life's challenges cause set-backs but we can't stop; we have to "keep it moving" no matter what. We have to trust God and allow Him to help us become that virtuous woman that Proverbs 31:10-31 talks about. KIM provides empowering tools such as workshops, seminars, and trainings to help women get back on their feet and get reestablished so they can be better persons for their family, the church, and the community.

Kathy L. Cunningham
Keep It Moving…You Have A Destiny
keepitmoving365@gmail.com
(301) 752-7004

www.ingramcontent.com/pod-product-compliance
Lightning Source LLC
Chambersburg PA
CBHW072338300426
44109CB00042B/1783